Pearls of Wisdom:

Affirmations for Daily Living

Shelley -
Everyday is an
opportunity to know
yourself more
fully! ♡ Gina

Pearls of Wisdom:

Affirmations for Daily Living

By
Gina Hernandez Tabrizy, LMFT

Compassionate Publications
2019

Note: All the quotes have been borrowed from different internet websites.

First Printing: 2019
ISBN:978-0-359-90057-2

Compassionate Publishing
23173 La Cadena Dr
Laguna Hills, CA 92653

www.compassionatepublications.com

Dedication

This book was born out of fear and necessity. I have always felt I had something to say and to share that was meaningful and had value; that could help others on the journey of life. However, the toxic voice of fear has stopped me over and over again from putting my words to paper, until one day I thought, I write on Facebook every day without fear and in hope of inspiring others, and I've gotten feedback over and over that my words were helping someone. One person encouraged me over and over again, and when he published his own book, he once again inspired me to be fearless and take those words of mine to print: my husband Farid. Thank you, sweetheart, for your tireless support of me, my vision, my life, for always encouraging me and bringing out my best self, for never giving up on me at my lowest points, and for being my biggest fan, protector, and love. To you I am eternally grateful for making this dream a reality.

To my children for teaching me that life is not meant to be a linear sequence of tasks to achieve so as to achieve acceptance, but a journey to be ridden like a rollercoaster, hanging on, letting go, screaming and laughing through the ups and downs. You have colored outside the lines and taught me that I can do the same. You are my greatest teachers. I am always proud of who you are and to be called your mom. Talia I absolutely love your cover drawing, it was exactly what I pictured! Thank you for doing this for me! Cez, thanks for gathering all the quotes from my pages too!

To my father for teaching me to never give up and that I can do anything I put my mind to, and for always loving me.

To my mother for teaching me that the best gifts come from giving your gifts away; you taught me to care for others.

Testimonials

"Thank you so much. You have no idea how you have impacted my views of life tonight. Love you. You are bad ass!!"

"I can't wait till your book comes out!!! You are 1 amazing woman and I enjoy your lives so much I have severe depression and anxiety both and listening to you speak really is amazing!!! Xoxo"

"I have watched every one of your videos on "Ask Gina" & on "Wings of Encouragement". I wanted to say "Hello", because you do not even know I exist, and how much you have helped me!! You have totally been a God Send to me!! You have made such a complete difference in my life!! I was praying to God, about needing mentors and people who encourage me to take me to the next levels in my life...and then I was led to you!! I have been in a low spot of my life and needed your encouragement to help keep me going!! I wanted you to know I think the world of you and appreciate all you are doing to help our communities!! You are so amazing and I feel that God is truly using you as an instrument!! I love how real you are, and that you have no pretense!! I appreciate your transparency in opening up and being vulnerable in sharing who you are!! You are a beautiful human being!! Do not stop what you are doing and have confidence in the fact that you are helping so many people that you do not even know exist!! We need you and so appreciate you, and I wanted to tell you that you are so loved!! You are truly amazing!! I cannot wait to see you and learn more about myself as I journey inward and move forward through life!! You have explained lifelong answers that I have searched for and never found, and as I listen the lightbulb comes on for me. I have been working hard on me, and am trying to move forward to a healthy and whole place in my life!! I just wanted to encourage you and let you know without a doubt, how much you are needed and loved in this world!! Keep doing what you are doing, you are making a huge impact on all of us out here!! We need to hear your voice, your heart, your knowledge and your experience!! You ARE saving lives!! ❤ ❤ ❤"

Be the Unicorn

Be the Unicorn, what does this mean? In a world of conformity, media marketing who and what we should be, what's acceptable and "normal", be the unicorn! Dare to stand out, to break from the pack, to speak your truth in the face of fearing others criticism or rejection. Tell your story, all the parts of it, the good the bad and the ugly, let people see you and know that you're not perfect, that you have bad days as you have good. Seeing the incredible reaction to my putting out my depression, one more time, and in much more detail, I see how little people knew this part of my story. Telling your story is healing! I dare to be seen and hope it inspires you to be seen!

55 and still alive! Grateful for every day I still get to be on the planet, always believing that I'm only here to do good and be a beacon of hope to those who suffer. Grateful to the friends and family that have celebrated with me and my beautiful Facebook friends who walk with me on my journey. Celebrate your birthday and celebrate your life. This is all you have, this moment, this opportunity to feel alive and embrace all that life can offer you. Go out and grab it! You are the only you in the universe! Celebrate that! Much love to you!

Self-Love:

The act of self-love often misunderstood as selfishness or narcissism. To love one's self means to begin the journey of being human. To accept the creation that is you with all your pitfalls and pleasantries. To know that you are worthy and deserving of love, no matter what you were taught, or told, no matter if you don't believe it. Speaking to yourself as a gentle mother or friend always loving, encouraging, and believing in you. Take notice of how you patronize or minimize yourself throughout your day and knock it off! You cannot feel love and experience joy when you are constantly doubting yourself! That critical voice is just a memory of other people's words towards us, and not actually our own. Speak lovingly to yourself and you will begin to feel lovingly towards yourself.

Worth is not the value of a possession but the measure of the value you attribute to it, know your own worth, you are invaluable!

Just 5 minutes a day, close your eyes and let go of everything and allow yourself to feel all the privileges you have received and still do every day.

Legacy:

I'm still taking in the loss of your presence on this planet. Some people come to make a ripple or a wave, you my friend came to make a Typhoon. Your journey and story of recovery brought many people to the path of healing! There is no greater measure of a human than the impact they make on others' lives. Yours will be felt for decades! May your heart be full of the knowledge you have lived well and your soul soar in the heavens! May this be a legacy we all leave behind!

Upon return to my routine I noticed this underlying anxiety that started to mount. I realized it was going from zero to hundred without a warm-up. Noticing that feeling, I realized I have to work just as hard at taking breaks and breathers in my day as I do at being productive. Taking time out to breathe and refuel is no joke! Reducing stress has great advantages to your health!

Don't bleed on others:

This is simple yet powerful and true! The parts of you that have gone unchecked and unrecovered will act and react towards others out of emotional immaturity caused by a lack of awareness of self. Heal yourself and you will not bleed on others. Focus on yourself and how you can change your responses to things that upset you, instead of thinking you can change others and how they respond to you. You are powerless over others but have full capacity to heal yourself.

Enveloped in beauty, one's spirit is relaxed and renewed. The ocean has such a healing energy, a sense of calm, and a reminder of how very small we are compared to its vastness.

I don't seek perfection, I seek to be the best version of myself and share that with the world! If my world is my family, friends, peers, colleagues, and clients then that is a vast world amongst itself, and it is enough! Do not only be yourself, but share yourself with others so that your legacy live on!

Don't worry:

"Don't worry about a thing, cause every little thing going to be all right!" Breathe into your anxiousness/worry about whatever is ailing you and repeat this phrase. You are bigger than your circumstance and you can triumph over it! "Don't worry; be happy". Be gentle with yourself and treat yourself with kindness and compassion today, I challenge you! Worry never won a race or a Presidency; determination, belief, and action made that happen! Worry doesn't change the future it only brings pain to the present. So breathe and let go, and state: just for today, I will not worry.

There is something magical about traveling! Leaving the place of routine and familiarity and launching into the unknown, peculiar, and spontaneous realm of a foreign country. Allow yourself to explore what's outside your common borders. Heaven is a vast and infinite universe of splendor, awaiting exploration.

Exercise for Life:

Always my happy place is at the gym! I started working out when I was 14 years old and I have never ever stopped! I would read fitness magazines, run the lake by my childhood home, do sit ups and pushups in my room, until 18 when I got hired as a fitness instructor for Elaine Powers, the female Jack Lalane. Then I really fell in love with fitness. The camaraderie of a group moving together to one purpose, feeling good; getting healthy. I love the feeling of challenging myself, pushing limits, and being strong. I've earned a second-degree Black Belt in Tae Kwon Do and taught Kickboxing for years. During my cancer I had the gym to look forward to and a way to measure that I was strong in spite of it. When I battle depression, working out is my relief. My friends have wondered about how I have stayed fit as I age, and this is it. Dedication to the pursuit of health and happiness. Nothing worth doing ever comes easy, but the gains are tremendous. Exercise teaches mindfulness, staying present, facing challenges, elevating your mood, and healing your body. It's not so much how you look but how you feel that's the goal.

There's this feeling of peace when you come to a place where you feel open enough to give and receive love. Tell yourself that each day you can embrace a feeling of calm surrender and invite the love of others to wrap around you.

Dragonfly:

The dragonfly, in almost every part of the world symbolizes change and change in the perspective of self-realization; the kind of change that has its source in mental and emotional maturity and the understanding of the deeper meaning of life. He came to sit upon my shoulder and I recognized in that small stillness something meaningful did occur. "Not all of us can do great things, but we can do small things with great love."- Mother Teresa.

As I walked up to the hospital to visit my husband's aunt in a fragile state, I am reminded to do everything with love. See, we are estranged from this family and the expectation is not there that we should come. However, doing what is right is not done for others but for yourself. For your self-worth, for your self-esteem, for your soul! In so doing you pray that others might see your love and receive it; pray they be changed by it, but even if not, do what is right anyway.

You Are Not Your Past:

Near and dear to my heart: don't let others judge you by your past; just because they haven't turned the page to who you are now, doesn't mean you shouldn't! You are not your experiences; they are part of your story and serve to guide and teach but they are not you. You are a living breathing essence existing in this very moment, embrace this person right now, right as you are.

Every day, and in every way, let's lift each other up as people. We don't have to unite just in our brokenness, our abuses, or loss of rights, but in our triumphs, our successes, our joys. Be happy for your sisters and brothers who earn that crown; praise them, for they are leading the way.

When people hold resentment, they're losing the gift that comes from releasing it; forgiveness.

Sharing:

We had an amazing time sharing our stories of our work, our passion, and our recovery. We opened up our space to welcome new energy, new care partners, and new possibility. Always open your heart and your home, your work, for the opportunity to give back and share what you have. If you believe in something strongly stand up for it and show people what matters most to you!

If in your childhood you were made to feel less than, you will

seek out relationships that will validate this. Drugs and alcohol

will help you choose the worst relationships of your life.

Addiction is a fearless search, an infinite search for joy, for passion, unfulfilled.

Find Your Tribe:

I have these women in my life now who elevate and celebrate me! It's not about competing or comparing to one another, it's about enjoying each other's special and unique gifts. I'm grateful for their friendships and how it adds to the quality of my life. Grateful my friend took the time to throw a Friendsgiving celebration for us all! Find your tribe of people whom whenever in your presence you feel your spirit lifted with joy and centered with peace. It will be time well spent.

If you are always seeking the approval of others, you are missing out in accepting the one person you can do anything about, yourself.

Demons Within:

The demon of depression has crawled upon my back once again. This dark insidious beast consumes my thoughts and energy, making me feel small, lost, and alone. I look to the horizon to be inspired by something greater than this to remind myself that I am part of this universe not separate from it, that I am meant to find my divine purpose and not have it robbed by this thief that has no face and bares no soul. Do not be reduced by your circumstance, your affliction - be it mental health, physical disease, financial deprivation, or loss of any kind. You absolutely have the right to heal and be free of this, hold your head up look to the sun I too will be gazing with you. I see you, and now you see me! Grateful for this special moment captured here to remind me of a better day!

How you speak to yourself changes how you feel! No matter what, feed your mind thoughts that uplift you.

You are born worthy of love, don't let anyone diminish

your right to it.

Singing in the Rain:

I'm "singing in the rain, just singing in the rain". Not! I've always noticed how directly I'm impacted by the weather, when the light dims, I seem to dim. This is common for many people and has generated a diagnosis known as Seasonal Affective Disorder. (SAD, of course). There are always ways to combat these feelings. One is get up and move, even if you can't get out in the areas you are in, find some activity at home to keep you moving. Call a friend and share your feelings or make plans to meet up; if you need to, do it on Skype/FaceTime. Sometimes just taking a nap to let yourself rest and the feelings pass helps. Watch or listen to something inspirational, music. Tell yourself this is just a moment, it too shall pass; I will feel better! Don't surrender to what doesn't serve you! Sing, sing in the rain! Sending love!

Holding on to a moment of grace; of peace, a reminder of the greater importance of the day. Of not getting caught up in the very trivial, and holding on to the greater purpose of life. Simply love, in all things, in all ways.

Perspective:

Your perspective can define how you live your life. If you believe that this moment is all you have and live it with every ounce of your being, then what is coming doesn't matter, and it can't define you. Be in this moment like you don't know if you will live another day.

When will we recognize that those who are terrorizing us are our own mentally ill? Mental illness is an epidemic just as addiction is. We need to inform ourselves to see the signs, but more important than that is to get treatment. If you see someone who suffers, or worry because someone's behavior has dramatically changed and you have fear or concern, reach out and ask for help. Our silence is deadly.

Mothering:

As a mother of children I've birthed, children I haven't but adopted in my heart, countless adults who I've mothered who didn't have the mother they needed, and fur babies too; I whole-heartedly affirm that being a mother is not reserved for those who give birth, but for all those who open their heart and take in the homeless, motherless, children, adults, humans, and animals alike who roam our earth in need of being mothered.

No one is immune to struggle and heartache. Decide to rise
above your defeat; do not let it define you or limit you, you
deserve to be the hero of your story!

Give love, attract love:

I'm always happy when I get to spend time with her! She's funny, warm, loving, kind, and a big sap like me! My boss is da bomb! When you give love you attract love and this is magnetic! Work is a joy not a chore and I wish that everyone could feel like that! Even work, especially work because it consumes a lot of our time, should be approached with love. Think about being loving to every person you encounter through the day, the checkout person, the elevator passenger, the neighbor, the co-worker, the boss. As you give and reflect love the energy around you shifts and you feel lighter so do those around you. Ever notice the Eeyore at your job, always seeing what's wrong and not what's right? They are so draining to be with, so be the opposite and lift up energy instead of sucking it dry.

Choose wisely and choose well, your heart is drawn to those whose hearts beat as your own, don't stay where you don't feel more alive.

Struggle:

Every struggle will manifest an opportunity for deeper connection within yourself, to explore the demons within and face what is inevitable! Then and only then will you make a choice to fight and face your truths or continue in the struggle! Don't ever quit. You and I have the right to be victorious over our struggle!

Do not keep nurturing relationships which are robbing you of joy.

Fear is a challenge to face what I have been resisting.

Laughable:

My funny valentine...

Sweet, comic valentine...

You make me smile with my heart

Your looks are laughable, un-photographable

yet you're my favorite work of art...

Enough said, sometimes a song speaks to you this one spoke to me. But I don't think your looks are laughable honey, but you always make me laugh.

Treasure those who make you laugh out loud and not take life so seriously.

We all need comic relief!

Do not let others diminish your worth, you are more than enough.

One of the happiest moments in life is when you find the courage to let go of what you cannot change.

Holidays:

It is not wrapped in a package or tied with a bow, it's is not hidden in a closet or under a tree; it is a feeling of love, joy, and celebration of all that is and is yet to be! This is the spirit of Christmas and all the holidays. It is time for pause and reflection. It is time to remember the value of other human beings, and how they enrich our lives. A time to forgive and realize the preciousness of time and how quickly it passes. It is a time to take in your surroundings and see how truly blessed you are in this moment. Whatever ails you or whatever burden you are carrying, focus on what you still have - not what you don't.

Your value doesn't decrease based on someone's inability to

see your worth.

Stop hating yourself for everything you are not. Start loving yourself for everything that you are.

Miracles:

My recovery has taught me to be bold and not fear my emotions but embrace them. Even the darkest of them I believe are part of a divine purpose for me to never stop growing nor believing in Miracles. Coming out of the dark I see and feel coming back to me all the love, positivity, and support I have put out into the universe. I'm immensely grateful for those who read my struggle and sent love support prayers and guidance; those that held my hand or shared a meal. Being there for another human who struggles is the greatest difference you can make in the world, which has a ripple effect on all other human beings!

Do you speak to your partner, parent, or friend the way you wish them to speak to you? Be the example of what you need.

Anyone can show up when things are easy, true friends show up when times are tough.

Forgiveness:

Yesterday was a day of reflection, grief through the loss of another of our elders. I saw in her, that her greatest gift was forgiveness. We are all imperfect humans and often just an amalgam of who others expect us to be. Can't we simply forgive our imperfect humanness? Can my friend forgive the ocean for taking her greatest love? Can the Moon forgive the sun for rising? With love all these things are possible. Embrace the loss, hold it dear, for deep in its bowels is love, and love forgives all things.

Authenticity takes courage. Be courageous, your spirit is calling

for it.

New Year:

It's not always hoopla and fanfare ringing in the New Year, sometimes it's bittersweet, some sadness for things lost or gone by. Remember a day that was magical, one for me, where you laughed till you cried, you felt you were at your best, you felt loved, then hold that moment dear and let it wash away any sorrow of today for tomorrow is a New Year! Thank you to all of you who have walked this journey with me this past year, celebrated my life, and listened to my grief as well. Thank life for every gift it has bestowed you and those yet to come. Believe in something greater than yourself and know that you have all you need to heal.

Don't give up when something is hard, that's when you are building your emotional muscles.

Grief:

There will always be grief, fear and loss. In the middle of that grief look for gratitude, it is not easy, but it is possible! When you lose a loved one what do you imagine they would feel if they saw you lost in your grief? Think about how they would want you to live, and for them this is how you honor their memory.

Know within yourself that you will not fall to your circumstances, your fears, your doubts, or your pain! Stay! Stay inside yourself invincible: "I will triumph", "I am a fighter"!

This Too Shall Pass:

Sometimes nature puts on a magical show for us to see; we just have to stop long enough to look and catch her glory. When you can't find the answer on the ground look up to the heavens, see how small your problem is in the face of the infinite sky, and believe this too shall pass! The outdoors reminds us of the connection of all living things, and to pause and take it in to our soul. Look outside find a tree, a bird, a blue sky, a green grass, a meadow, a puddle of water, a stone; each a remembrance of how wondrous the world can be, and how small our problems in the face of it.

Don't be afraid to change; change is the reminder you are growing and still alive.

Don't worry about what people say behind your back. They're

the ones who find faults in your life instead of fixing their own.

Numbing the Pain:

Addiction is about filling up a void; understanding that emptiness fuels the desire to consume is key! Start by noticing the feeling in the pit of your stomach, an ache, a loneliness; a sense of shame, doubt, and sadness. As that feeling rises into your chest in your heart it rushes a signal in the brain to STOP, to make this pain go away. That is the obsession in the mind of the addict who seeks anything outside themselves to self-soothe and dull the pain. The work is to begin to feel and grieve this pain and the story by which it was created. To begin to tolerate the pain so that it can be released and healed. Each day that you learn tolerance is a day you don't have to numb the pain.

Stop being afraid of what could go wrong and think of what could go right.

What is Possible:

I believe this for all of us: We are only limited by what we tell ourselves. When we strive for change, to follow a dream or passion, the only thing in our way is telling ourselves what we lack instead of what we are worth. Be your best coach in the New Year and talk to yourself like you would a friend or a child, with love, kindness, belief, and hope for what is possible. Don't set expectations for the New Year; just think of possibilities for it. Every day is a new day for you to reinvent yourself.

Sometimes courage means knowing when to stay silent, sometimes it's knowing when to be heard.

Just Stay:

When the cold sets in, find a window of warmth; a place of calm and quiet reflection. When trouble or sadness come, don't feed them; take a pause, a deep breath, and look for the bright spot, the smallest thought of gratitude to penetrate the darkest moment. You can direct your steps, your path to tomorrow, if you just stay open to the possibility that the sun will shine again. Just stay; this too shall pass!

No one has the right to abuse you verbally, physically, or spiritually. Their abuse is not a measure of who you are; it's a measure of who they are.

Individuate:

The truth is knowing your partner is not everything. Not expecting that they fulfill your every whim and desire. You have your own unique, distinct and separate identities. Your partner is there to support and nurture your dreams, desires, and interests but doesn't have to agree with or cater to these. When you flourish as an individual you bring energy to the relationship and enthusiasm for life and that fuels your partner's own passions!

When the year comes to a close, don't look behind you; turn around and look ahead, that's where you are heading. Take with you a renewed sense of wonder and joy for this moment, and every moment, for this moment is your life.

No one deserves to feel imprisoned in a relationship. Love does

not hold hostages.

See the Good:

Look back and hold on to the good. Let go of the bad. Let go of what doesn't serve you! See what good people do and what they offer you. Don't hold on to what they don't do and where they fail you. In the end we are all human; fragile and imperfect! Joy comes from accepting what is, not resisting what isn't!

Do you fear success because somehow you don't believe you are that wonderful? Or that you truly deserve it? Stop discounting your worth!

Resentment:

Recognize what you need to let go of, and actively release it! Resentment does not end by repeating it and talking about it over and over again. It's holding you hostage to the pain it creates in you and the people you think caused it. They go on living without a thought of it! Let go and live in peace.

In the middle of facing trauma when it's dark and you feel stuck, that's when you are in a cocoon transforming from a caterpillar to a butterfly.

You Are OK:

Sometimes you're just ok sitting in your own skin, in your life, in this moment! And sometimes you feel absolutely lost, confused, not knowing what to do or where to go or who to be. So hang on; hang on to those moments that feel right as rain, when there is nothing else you need to do or be and everything seems to line up in your favor. We can't know every day, in every moment, that we are divinely right where we are meant to be, so we struggle or suffer. When those blessed moments come, remember them; treasure them. They are there to remind us that everything is ok.

Whether we want it to or not, our presence has an effect! Even our shadow makes a difference. Nature doesn't even try to create and yet makes a divine impression. Be like the shadow, like nature, and leave an impression wherever you roam.

Fear:

Fear is the fire that fuels our hatred. Fear of people who are different, fear of the unknown, fear of what we don't understand, and fear of not being a part of something. Our fears have been passed down from our ancestors, our cultures, our religions, and our countries. Fear is an emotion that drives us apart. When we can instead allow love to be our driving force we are acting from our most basic human instinct and we will then act humanely. Love your neighbor as yourself!

Most of the difficulties we encounter in relationships with others comes from our lack of ability to directly communicate our thoughts and feelings to the person that we are trying to relate with in some way. Our perceptions of others' intentions towards us can very often be skewed. Try understanding before criticizing and you will build compassion instead of resentment.

Home:

There are these rare moments when you meet people that just feel like home. When this happens while I'm working, I feel doubly blessed. Your people are not where you think they should be or who you think they should be! Your people are those who warm your heart from the first time you meet them, who embrace you like you've known each other your whole life, and who celebrate and elevate your gifts. I found some of my people last week, keep your eye out for yours!

Holding on to a moment of grace, of peace, a reminder of the greater importance of the day...of not getting caught up in the very trivial... and holding on to the greater purpose of life. Simply love, in all things, in all ways.

Trauma:

Addiction is the perfect partner to fill the void trauma leaves in you. You use substances to fill the pain. That pain is an empty well that will never be filled. You can't heal from your trauma by avoiding it.

Don't stay where you are not wanted, cherished, or regarded.

Rough Morning:

So along with the rains I caught a cold I had trouble shaking and today I have a little medical procedure for a side effect of the medication I take for cancer prevention! You know all those lovely commercials about curing one thing that causes 25 others? This is one of those scenarios. Every obstacle brings with it an opportunity to seize the moment; to get inspired to not waste time with what you are powerless over! I know my time is precious and I want to make a difference in whatever way I can. I write this to you today to inspire you to get up and keep fighting for your purpose! How can you make a difference today?

Trauma occurs when your basic needs go unmet leaving a wound that seeks to be fulfilled.

Moments:

An afternoon of Hope! At a moment of vulnerability and sorrow, I was lifted up by being of service and being in the presence of so many who were being of service to support the homeless and give back to the beautiful women and children I serve at <u>New Directions for Women</u> every day! Thank you to <u>Hired Power</u> and <u>Capstone</u> for bringing the community together!

Friendships are built over time with dedication to the invitation of togetherness, celebration, affection, and attention. All those worth making require tending, so tend to your friendships as the tulips in your garden for they will blossom and grow!

Purpose:

I am living with purpose and am loving my purpose; to give what I have, to stand behind what I believe, to speak the truth and use that truth to inspire others. Words are the pearls of my treasure and I share them one by one with those who will listen, and those who are listening grow each day.

The less you respond to negativity, the more peaceful your life becomes.

If I Ruled the World:

If I ruled the world, it wouldn't matter what you have; what you give that would count. Status is a perception that where I sit is somehow going to protect me from falling from grace.

Acting as if everything will be all right is training your brain to accept that something better is coming rather than succumbing to a moment of despair. Love yourself in spite of your circumstances and believe you can triumph!

Release:

Anger is a natural emotion that seeks a physical release; hold your tongue and move your body. Whether it's walking or boxing or any other physical outlet, it will allow you to release pent up emotions and find a more balanced and healthy way of being.

The worst person to be around is a person who complains about everything and appreciates nothing.

Joy:

Well this is how to start a Birthday right! Good friends, a beautiful hike, great conversation, plenty of laughter and some bad ass wigs!! This so perfectly captures seeking the joy in life and the joy of just being with your sisters. Let yourself laugh till you cry, and shed a couple tears of joy! My soul sisters: I love you and you bring me joy! Beyond grateful for this and you!! Celebrate yourself for there will never be another you.

Embrace those around you and love them for the gifts they

bear, not the expectations you have of them.

You Are Not Alone:

Life is not a journey we are supposed to take alone. One way to find solace and create joy is by finding those people that lift your spirit simply by being in their presence. Many years I spent weeding through half-measured friendships, half-hearted relationships, searching for people that could be my tribe. Your soul gravitates towards those it recognizes as home. So glad to be home! Grateful again for the outpouring of love towards my post last week on my struggle with depression. Sending love and healing to anyone who may be feeling the same.

Take an inventory of where you have been hurt in relationship and how to move forward! Don't stay stuck in your past. Share with someone you need to hear this message!

I believe no one ever gets to tell you who you are, because

they will always get it wrong.

Staycation:

A "staycation" staying not too far from home and when the rain and wind start to rise, staying indoors and getting some much needed rest. Give yourself permission to stay! Stay in respite, stay in relaxation, stay in recovery and healing. Stay close to what lifts your spirit and move away from what doesn't. Take a staycation often!

The joy and sorrow of being a mother is knowing you love your children more than they can possibly ever imagine loving you, and missing them every second of every day they are away from you! May your joy be greater than your grief today, and may your grief see its final day in your heart.

The Struggle is Real:

As I battle depression and I share on my bad days the pain it may cause me, I also always share the hope for a better day. By believing in that possibility I will myself see the light and the silver lining. Your mind accepts what you tell it, especially if it is for your own good. I hope you see that in a hard day I keep believing there's a better day coming! Whatever struggle you are in keep believing you can be liberated from it! Stay focused on what beauty and love is present in your life right now and embrace it.

Taking a personal inventory means a fearless search for the truth inside yourself, a soul search, to discover the darkness that came before the addiction and free yourself of the shame of it.

Deeper Connection:

"Lady sings the Blues"... but not this lady and not today! Today we shared stories of our lives, journeys of our current lives, of age, of families, of heartache, of reuniting, of standing your ground! For three hours we sat just captivated by each other's simple and honest narrative of our lives. At one point laughing that we needed some popcorn because it was like a movie! Dare to have in depth conversations with your friends where you truly reveal yourself and not just the surface mask that is mostly worn to adhere to social niceties. We all are living lives of 3 dimensions and sharing those other shades brings a deeper sense of connection and peace within yourself!

Wherever you are in this moment know that you are worthy, you have value just for breathing, and lift yourself up! Rise! Rise to the occasion, face the day, the dilemma, the disease, the struggle, head on. Don't fear moving forward fear staying where you are unhappy, unloved, unnoticed. There are these divine moments where you are elevated; lifted up to your divine purpose. Rise to that occasion!

Speak to a Stranger:

When people lift you up instead of put you down, you can accomplish so much more. These two beautiful people met me because we sat by each other at a restaurant. Because we chose to share a space and began to share a conversation, we discovered we had in common the nationality of our Cuban-born fathers, and from their immense understanding a kinship formed! We talked for hours like we were best friends! At the end of which they spontaneously just lifted me up. We are all "6 degrees of separation". Speak to a stranger and you may find a friend!

Fear often masks anger and anger often masks fear.